T0149850

The Year the Eggs Cracked

The Year the Eggs Cracked

Poems

J DIEGO FREY

A Division of Samizdat Publishing Group

CONUNDRUM PRESS A Division of Samizdat Publishing Group.
PO Box 1279, Golden, Colorado 80402

The Year the Eggs Cracked.

Copyright © 2015 by J Diego Frey.

All rights reserved. Printed in the United States of America. No part
of this book may be used or reproduced in any manner whatsoever
without written permission except in the case of brief quotations
embodied in critical articles and reviews.

For information, email INFO@CONUNDRUM-PRESS.COM.

ISBN: 978-1-942280-24-8

Library of Congress Control Number: 2015931343

Conundrum Press books may be purchased with bulk discounts for
educational, business, or sales promotional use. For information
please email: info@conundrum-press.com

Conundrum Press online: conundrum-press.com

Gratitude and love is expressed to my family, who keep me searching for new ways to describe what it's like to live with them. Thank you, Sarah, Henry, and Lydia—you are all in here. And so is that bad cat as well.

Many thanks to my teachers at Lighthouse Writers Workshop, particularly Michael Henry, Chris Ransick, and Joy Sawyer. Thank you also to the students of the Lighthouse Youth Writers poetry classes, who have taught me more about poetry than I them.

It bears grateful mention also that at least a few of the poems contained herein were previously published in prestigious literary journals.

- "Ted's Shirt" appeared in the inaugural issue of the short-lived *Battery Journal*, 1999, from San Francisco.

- "Amorous Elk in Underpants" appeared (under an alternate title) in the 2012 issue of *Huge Underpants of Gloom*.

- "Rejected David Lynch Plotlines (in Haiku)" appeared in the Spring 2012 issue of *A Capella Zoo*.

- "Emily Launches Diego" appeared in the 2013 issue of *Don't Just Sit There*.

- "Gas Cap Gas Cap Ashtray Grill" is included in *Write, I See*, published in 2014 by the Denver Art Students League.

For Annette, who first clued me in to all this

TABLE OF CONTENTS

Part One: FILLER

Part Two: MADRID

Part One: FILLER

"I am food. I am food. I am the eater of food."

—from The Upanishads

The Next Two Words Are Just Filler

but not the words
"are just filler"

or even the word
"words"

just the words "next two,"
because they were
the next two words.

Freshness Statement

We guarantee
that all the ideas
conceits
twisted syntax
phraseology
emotional rubiconage
pe-dego-logical references
and rabid barks
contained herein
were made up fresh
not that far away
and no more than
five lifetimes prior
to this moment
right now,
in which you, happy consumer,
ripped open
the plastic seal
with an audible
inrush of outside air
and pulled out this poem
still damp
from the entirely
original
tears of its author.

The Reason that Can Be Reasoned is Not the Eternal Reason, the Name that Can Be Named is Not the Eternal Name

The weasel that can be weaseled
is not the eternal weasel.

The nose that can be nosed
is not the eternal nose.

The burger that can be cheeseburged
wears not its coat of cheese well.

The humble ho-ho that can be hoed
will eternally be hosed.

The eternal ass
can't be assessed with twenty-twenty vision.

The last rose standing
in eternity will have never really risen.

Thus and here it is: You can
get what you want, but, it's silly—
you'll have never really gotten it,
not what you wanted, really.

A poker game that can be gamed
will never poke eternal.

And the eternal chicken
will not be chicked
by some cat named "the colonel."

Package

for S

Whenever two trains
one traveling at 50 miles per hour
in a westerly direction
and the other traveling
at 80 miles per hour
to the east meet
on a trestle bridge
high above a mountain stream
that itself is rushing south
at 20 miles per hour,
there should, of necessity,
be a single migrating goose
cut off from his flock
racing northward
at a remarkable 110 mph
across the sky above
in order to tie this picture
up into a neat package
that I could leave for you,
without fanfare,
on the breakfast table
where you will find it
when you get up
from bed and make your way
downstairs.

Triolet for Lucky

I wish
I was
an Oscar Meyer Wiener,

because some people
think hot dogs
are "awesome."

This life it keeps on
coming, round
and round to meaner.

So I wish
I was
an Oscar Meyer Wiener.

The world
would have me
every night for dinner,

and it would feel me
in its teeth
and run to floss them.

I wish
I was
an Oscar Meyer Wiener,

because some people
think hot dogs
are "awesome."

Yummy Fudge!

Leaving it aside for now
the fact that we're all doomed,

I want to tell you just how much
I truly love this fudge.

The road to hell is cleared of blocks,
its borders are well groomed.

But, let's leave that aside for now.
(We know that we're all doomed.)

The cantaloupes are screaming and
the mushroom clouds have bloomed.

This world of ours is stomped and saddened,
swamped with storm and grudge.

But leaving it aside for now
this fact that we're all doomed,

I feel the need to call attention
to this very yummy fudge!

Amorous Elk in Underpants

I was there,
and it's important
that you know the events
as they truly transpired,
with the ripped dress,
the oversized boxer shorts,
and the discarded rack of elk antlers.

A number of accounts
are focusing on the antlers.
Why were they discarded?
Just what was the state of mind
of the bull elk who was found
bugling lewdly from a nearby clearing?

But this is outside the point. You see,
poor Mrs. Weatherwell tore her dress on the door
fleeing from my cabin,
not in disgust (as has been my experience in the past),
but in shame.

I had rejected her offer
to "have sex out in the open,
as the wild ungulates do."

Understand, I like Mrs. W.
I'd be more than happy
to mate with her in the field,
listen to her grateful
ululations echoing back at us
from the mist-shrouded hills.

But it was too damn cold.

She didn't wait to ask me why.
She just turned
and abruptly galloped
out into the night

and eventually
to the ranger station,
there to concoct
that ridiculous story
about an amorous elk in underpants.

Fossilization Song

I do not wish in any way
to drive to Dinosaur today.

It's almost all the way to Utah
across that Western tray—
past the Rifles and Eagles
and the ungulates at play.

The sun is setting on this Tuesday,
Tyranno-Jesus how I pray:
Please don't make me make the drive
to Dinosaur today.

"Zen Exodus from a Tyrannosaurus Rex"

for Raja (or what I thought you said)

It's not like you can
ever really leave him.

It takes you twenty steps of leaving
for each one of his arriving.

And we cannot know just how
he explains the universe to himself.

Only that you will eventually separate
into two large wet pieces

and slip, largely untasted, past
the garage door of his epiglottis.

But, at last, I think that I get the significance
of the old monster's stubby stubby arms,

what they meant to him
and how you managed your last desperate attack

on the lizard king's image of himself,
flapping about as you did,

banging your own limbs with such hilarious impotence
on the locked outer door of our shelter.

Rejected David Lynch Plotlines (In Haiku)

Bob Dylan trips, falls
into fishtank. Must be saved
from anemone.

Romantic moment
in restaurant altered
by dying waiters.

Devil arrives home.
Can't find housekeys. Door transforms
into vagina.

You know what's funny?
Big wet dog, sudsy bath.
Name the pooch "Mozart."

Cut to pile of fish.
2 men climb out from under,
embrace weepily.

People start shrinking
but act like nothing's wrong as
house pets get bigger.

12 chimps dressed as men
enter red room. There are chairs,
but not enough chairs.

Beware of Don

In un-gentle tones
agreed upon
by both of you
in a document
you no longer
remember signing,
he will relate to you
graphic and
embarrassing
details
of his earlier
(read: "back on the farm")
sex life.

Colonoscopy: A Rhupunt

They'd rather peer
inside your ear
and leave your rear
the hell alone.

And as they mine
your sad behind
with probes unkind
your day is blown.

Look for cancer
while your pants are
down they answer
the telephone.

Ride the Pharaoh: A Tritina

We choose to attend the fair
and pay an expensive fare
to ride on something called the "Pharaoh."

Odd little ride, the "Pharaoh,"
an experience far from fair,
yet strangely, we were glad we paid the fare.

Just one large silver coin is the fare.
And for that you are treated like a pharaoh.
Revered, then mummified, and buried in a tomb far
    beneath the fair.

If you're still at the fair, come pay the fare, and join us at rest
    with the "Pharaohs."

Softball Bat: A Tritina

The six-foot man who calls himself "Batman"
swings up too late for his turn at bat, man.
At dusk, the air fills with bats.

Softball teams shrink from the bats,
as does the pigeon-toed man who calls himself "Batman."
He screams—a high-voiced shriek like a bat, man.

The bats are only after bugs, though. Not bat, man,
nor any of us are in fact in danger from the bats.
Yes, not even the crying little boy who calls himself "Batman."

Oh, weeping "Batman," pick up your bat, man, and disappear
into the dark like the bats.

Postcard from Pyongyang

Kim Jong Il
and my friend Phil
went shopping
for some weed.

Phil got ill
from smoke infill
and Jong choked
on a seed.

Kim Jong Il
smoked chlorophyll
that smelled like
what Phil peed.

Phil agreed
and Jong conceded
that Il should still
just chill.

Heart of Chert

Only two more days 'til doomsday,
almost time to change my shirt.

Been sleeping with my clothes on
since my baby left with Bert.

Those horses of Apocalypse
should ride him 'til it hurts.

Been sleeping close to doomsday
since my baby left with Bert.

Nobody likes an empty bed tho'
and the best of us revert . . .

I'll be sleeping close to Ernie
now that baby's left with Bert.

It's not the same still, and will not be
'til he's dead beneath the dirt.

My baby meant the world to me
tho' she never liked our yurt.

And the world means nothing to me now.
My heart becomes inert.

So, I'm gonna move to Maine with Ernie
since baby left with Bert.

Which Divides Us

This is, she said,
less of a barrier
less boundary
than the razor-fine line
that separates a cheerio
from a honey-nut cheerio

and just as wide a gap at that.

Last Run of the Utah Brides

The Utah brides
they did it all
Winnie, Mavis
Trixie, Moll.
I tried to marry
every one
as had my forebear
B. H. Young.

Trixie had a taste
like strong tequila
in a shoe
and she rocked
aloud with laughter
when I showed her
my tattoo.

Mavis cooked
a breakfast
from the paste
of anchovies
but she set me
on the highway
cause my chest hair
made her sneeze.

Moll came dressed
for springtime
lemon bloomers
on her tush
we made love
just like a tractor
I would pull
and she would push.

Winnie was
the oldest
so I stayed
with her for keeps
She helps me
with my dentures now
and I grope her
while she sleeps.

The Utah brides
they did it all
Winnie, Mavis
Trixie, Moll.
Wished I could marry
every one
Be like my forebear
B. H. Young.

What I Want the Aliens to Do

The next time those aliens land in our town
I hope that they kidnap Dave T. from the bank.
He's been such an asshole to me all around . . .
So the next time the aliens land in our town,
if they could abduct him, yank his pants down,
and if not outright probe him, at least deliver a spank.
The next time those aliens land in our town
I hope they kidnap my boss, Dave, from the bank.

Stardust

Inside every favor there sits a small curse.
The sexiest smile eventually turns stiff.
True love is bad, obligation is worse.
Inside every favor there sits a small curse.
So for now let's make out in the back of your hearse—
let the time, and our lives, and the continents drift.
Inside every favor there sits a small curse.
The sexiest smile eventually turns stiff.

Gas Cap Gas Cap Ashtray Grill

after "Chevrolet" by Mark Friday

gas cap
gas cap
ashtray, grill

that time
I punched
the steering wheel

windshield wiper, differential
reclining
bucket seats

(necking
in the wrecking yard,
kisses tasted
like smoked meat)

silver, black, and burnt sienna
rattle of
an old antenna

from the turnpike's
windy blast

(the signal colors
of our past
and how those things
refused to last)

red lights
in the cracked rear glass

gas cap
gas cap
ashtray, grill

that time
I punched
the steering wheel

door frame
handbrake
spongy clutch

it nearly felt
as good to touch

your chrome

as it did
to drive
you home

Red Line

The old man
used to say
to me, "Boy,"

(I was
a boy then,
you see,)

"if you see
a red line,
glowing,
vertical,
in the center
of your enemy's
forehead,
don't wait.

"Strike fast
to the solar
plexus,
because
he is
about
to kill you."

The old man
was right,
much of the time.

Except that
some people
just kind of
have that line
all the time.

Even
in church.

Ted's Shirt

This is the plaid shirt that Ted wore.

These are the shoes that went with the plaid shirt that Ted wore.

This is the soap that washed off the dirt that covered the shoes that went with the plaid shirt that Ted wore.

This is the tune so soulful and rich, track five of the album that gave him the blues, on sale at the store that sold me the soap that washed off the dirt that covered the shoes that went with the plaid shirt that Ted wore.

This is the activity condemned by the Pope, practiced in closets and bedrooms and sinks, most often indulged in to nobody's hurt but awkward to be caught at on somebody's floor, that takes place to the tune so soulful and rich, track five of the album that gave him the blues, on sale at the store that sold me the soap that washed off the dirt that covered the shoes that went with the plaid shirt that Ted wore.

These are the conflicts that rise from beliefs of Germans and Bushmen and Muslims and Jews, in search of relief from some immortal itch for meaning and mercy and most often hope, who fight with each other over whose truth is whose, and what you should eat, and who heaven is for, in a ceaseless distraction of violence and hurt instead of the activity condemned by the Pope, that's practiced in closets and bedrooms and sinks, most often indulged in to nobody's hurt but awkward to be caught at on somebody's floor, that takes place to the tune so soulful and rich, track five of the album that gave him the blues, on sale at the store that sold me the soap that washed off the dirt that covered the shoes that went with the plaid shirt that Ted wore.

This is the eventual descent into chaos, an entropic
excitement of yellows and pinks as the world blows apart
from its mantle to core after one or another apocalypse
brews and submerges our Eden in so many griefs that they
can't be discarded like clothes in a ditch, to leave us at long
last standing nude and alert with an open perspective and
unlimited scope immune to the fear in control of the pathos,
the supermen master race heroes of lore who held on to
the fire while protecting the fuse that civilization retained
at it brinks as a warning to anyone unwilling to cope with
the upswell of conflicts that rise from beliefs of Germans
and Bushmen and Muslims and Jews, in search of relief
from some immortal itch for meaning and mercy and most
often hope, who fight with each other over whose truth is
whose, and what you should eat, and who heaven is for, in
a ceaseless distraction of violence and hurt instead of the
activity condemned by the Pope, that's practiced in closets
and bedrooms and sinks, most often indulged in to nobody's
hurt but awkward to be caught at on somebody's floor, that
takes place to the tune so soulful and rich, track five of the
album that gave him the blues, on sale at the store that sold
me the soap that washed off the dirt that covered the shoes
that went with the plaid shirt that Ted wore.

But It's Not Always about Me

I thought
that I was on to something
when my initials
floated past
in a bowl
(not mine)
of vegetable soup.

Part Two: MADRID

"No one in the world ever gets what they want,
and that is beautiful."
  —*from "Don't Let's Start," by They Might Be Giants*

Halcyon Jones

I miss the little things, like pills.
I miss the sunset on the Bay
and the fault beneath the Oakland hills.

I miss my neighbors Raj and Will,
who took me bowling and often paid.
I miss the little things, like pills.

The opium we smoked, the grill
on which we charred rich meat fillets.
I miss the fault of Oakland's hills.

I miss the times we'd hunt to kill
stalking underclassmen prey.
I miss the little things, like pills.

I miss the subtle twisted thrill
when Will and Raj both came out gay,
and blamed it on the Oakland hills.

And when the blood began to spill,
when jealous lust got in the way,
I missed the chance to grab the pills.

The past was better, better still
then this scarred Midwestern life today.
I miss the little things, like pills.
I miss the fault beneath the hills.

Never Summer Salad

Lost in time again
until tomorrow out
of reach beyond
furthest rhyme
for tarragon
we will still
be construing this soufflé
that once was meant to be our life together.

Tossed in lime
amidst the cilantro
and bloody distances
of the heart
we two souls
may marinate
to our eventual dissolution into each other.

Boston. I'm far
beyond the next
sunrise
and within
a man's perfect reach
for the final
clam to climb.

Sauced in thyme
and rosemary and wine,
crossed in the sublime crime
of not loving enough
yet wanting,
at all ends,
to be loved.

Flossed by mimes
and tossed to sleep
along the brine
and grime-slicked beach.

6 ½ Ways of Looking at a Jar of Eggnog

after Stevens

I
W/ all us twenty snowed-in neighbors
the only one moving
was the one without eggnog.

II
I was of two minds.
Which came first:
the egg, or the nog?

III
The eggnog whirled, not by blender
but with

IV
A man and a woman
drink one.
A man and a woman and an eggnog
arm wrestle.

V
Can't decide whether
I crave the beautiful
whiskey burn, like a rock song,
or the warm eggy belch afterwards.

VI
Ice cream, opened with
with a barbarous whisk
fills the bowl
before we cross it with eggnog.
The impenetrable beige
dairy, tracked with booze.

VII
O fat men of Highline,
why do you seek exotic after-dinner wines?
Can you not still taste
eggnog drunk from the homely
earth-shoes of your wives?

this fallout fantasy

after e e cummings

what if i
woke up and reno was gone
pulverized flat by a tumbleweed bomb?

much of the
misfits who stalk on the sand
would have wheels on their feet then and no thumbs on
their hand

which of a
wish for a perfect companion
would bring marilyn monroe in a jeep from the canyon?

wind
blows the blondes, though, too far from my reach
and my bones turn to oil
and the world to my beach

Watching Butch and Sundance at the Valley Drive-In

My dad reached out, unhooked the box,
and clipped it on the driver's side.
Dusty drive-in stretched for blocks.
My dad reached out, unhooked the box
so we heard Newman's tinny vox,
he and Redford's girl, a bike ride.
My dad reached out, unhooked the box
and clipped it on the driver's side.

Bad Dream about the First Day of Work

Involving too many manuals and not enough pants
and sinister coworkers who smell like asparagus.
They show you your desk, which is covered with sand
and too many manuals (and where are your pants?)
then mention the company's moving to France
(a fact which your co-workers think is hilarious).
You must pack up your manuals and locate some pants
and climb into a boat that just reeks of asparagus.

Memories of Villa Italia

after "Memorie di Villa Italia" (1961),
by Vance Kirkland

Sure, I remember Villa Italia.
It was a beautiful shopping experience.
800,000 square feet of consumabilia.
Yeah, I remember the Villa Italia.
Spencer's Gift with psychedelia,
Orange Julius and the fashion trends.
Sure, I remember Villa Italia.
It was a beautiful shopping experience.

The artist paints a different villa,
one that bleeds with lights and blooms,
with hieroglyphics and vanilla.
The artist dreams a different villa:
a home that could produce Godzilla
from any of its clouded rooms.
The artist paints a different villa,
one that bleeds with lights and blooms,

Perhaps the poet got it wrong.
One doubts the artist did.
To cast an oil paint in song . . .
perhaps the poet got it wrong.
He's not been at this very long . . .
in fact he's practically a kid.
Perhaps the poet got it wrong.
One doubts the artist did.

Emily Launches Diego: 4 Quatrains

—The leaves like women interchange
Behind the scenes of fall
But winter brings the sharpest change
When all those women fall

—Death is a conversation
Between the drinking and the up
There's future further down the stream—
But present's in my cup

—Let me not mar that perfect dream
Of you in underpants
In the kitchen whipping cream
And some erotic stance

—A thought went up my mind today
As a flag rams up a pole—
Flapped there in the breezy day
Of my once immortal soul

The End of Another Calendar, December 2012

A week, to the day, past the Mayan Apocalypse
and all of my neighbors are either dead or they're not.
The sky is still curled like an over-cooked taco chip
and plantar fasciitis is ruining my foxtrot.

These are days made of sacrifice and letting of blood
but that's not that much of a change from before.
The voters still fraud and the subways still flood.
The roof of my flat is still some monkey's floor.

Sure, I'm thinking of driving tomorrow downtown
body-painted in red paint and wearing a thong,
but it's not because some rules have flipped upside-down.
This has been behavior of mine all along.

My Siamese cat, Rick, is now revered as a god—
a station to which he has easily taken.
What's new though is how our door darkens with supplicants
crawling before him and offering him bacon.

Camelot Sneeze Dream

for A. Inman

I return to the scene of the crime
and you are waiting there
with a claw hammer in your purse
your pantsuit thick green
like an upholstered tree.

The moon looms
overhead
as if repelled
by your bouffant.

There is a song playing:
"Happy Birthday" in Russian.

I open a door.
I open a door.
Another door.
I open a door shaped like
your mother's hips
and step through.

A goodly stockpot
several Great Dane dogs
gathered around wearing party hats
lapping at reddish soup.

The soup sloshes onto the floor
dark, wet and sticky.
The sound of wind through a hole
in the far ceiling.

"We're in JFK's nose!"
you whisper excitedly,
twirling the claw hammer
over your head,
a utilitarian baton.

A small cluster of souls, tourists,
shuffles past.
A guide hurries them along,
shouting at their hunched heads,
"This way! This way!
We don't want to be late for the epiglottis!"

The floor ripples
and we all run in slow motion
toward a receding horizon of teeth.

I lose you in the confusion,
and when the sneeze comes, I am blind.

Area Man Dreams

I dreamt I was in my father's hotel suite at the family reunion but I couldn't lock the fancy glass door to the crapper.

I dreamt that the funny gay couple put the rest of us to shame with their advanced Swedish baby stroller, complete with advanced Swedish baby.

I dreamt I was playing touch football against a team made up of current and former therapy groups. They scored a touchdown on me with the ol' "everyone crawls down the field like a worm and you can't see who's lying on top of the ball" play.

I dreamt I had overslept in the rain.

I dreamt that too many neighbor children were on the roof, and that I couldn't seem to get them down by firing more children up there at them with my neighbor-children catapult. The neighbors were all coming home from their jobs at the big knife factory.

I dreamt that the toilet spoke to me in the voice of a regretful politician while backing up onto my shoes.

I dreamt of a tidal wave on the horizon made up of every unfinished project from every job I'd ever had—and I was still emptying the trash cans at the Fezwick Lake State Recreation Area, Summer of 1982.

I dreamt that my pants were too small for my head and my head was too big for the doorway to the space shuttle.

I dreamt that the Moon was downstairs, in the kitchen, waiting for an explanation.

Living Will

Sounds like "Living Bible."

It was covered
from Genesis to Zebra
in denim
because, "Hey man,
Fonzie-Jesus
wears jeans."

I am still convinced
that some things
are better left
as is.
That there is a right way
and a wrong.

So let me be clear:
if I awake from the operation a vegetable,
I wish to be sauteed
in olive oil
with garlic.

Not steamed.
And, for God's sake,
not served
in raw chunks—
with yogurt dip.

Twain

I got so caught up
trying to remember
that thing you said
about wintergreen—
how it is the most toothpaste of the candy flavors,

that I almost shoved out of
the other side of my mind
that thing
that I was trying
to remember to tell you
about that swollen
salmon-colored
sport ute
in the left lane ahead of me
all the way home on Santa Fe Drive.

Difficult to read its vanity plate
in the weak glow
of my dirty headlights
but it had read either "DINKY" or "OINKY."

And how there was no life
no twist of circumstances
that I could conceive of
in which I would feel able
to live up to that particular ride.

Two deeply, deeply trivial thoughts
that briefly shared ass-space
on the shallow bench
of my short-term memory

like some pair of idiot twins
arm-in-arm
waiting placidly
to catch the next bus to infinity.

The Nearly Nine Thousand Names of Onan

Something so private and yet so epiphanic
rarely gets talked about in a voice quite so serious.
Yet us happy cats who pursue this delirious
experience do with a zeal that can feel messianic.

The mythical prince in the land of self-love
never gets much respect up in angel-food heaven.
But on earth, we hosanna him seven-eleven
often while wielding a rabbit-fur glove.

I've heard self-abuse called the "one true religion,"
"a waltz in the swamp," or "the three-finger curl."
For a brief time in Brooklyn, I lived with a girlfriend
who called it "upsetting the pigeon."

Which sounds lovely to me, with its avian quicken
and something that only a woman could say.
Because for us men, the referenced playmate
must at least be the size of a fully grown chicken.

A farm bird is choked, a simian spanked,
a flag gets saluted, an academy thanked.
She might "drive to Nirvana in a little pink car,"
while he is next-door "playing one-string guitar."

The king in his underpants storms his own castle.
The queen runs amok in the pantry.
Somebody's rocket separates from the gantry.
Somebody's eel is earmarked for a hassle.

Because there's life and there's death it just goes that way
while our molecules vibrate along.
And the self that resists the invite to self-play
will never quite hear his own molecules' song.

We will "un-yoke the Yangtze," mount "Mount Suribachi."
We'll "Joanie the bologna" and "hibachi the Chachie."
With one-handed clapping sounds and "koaning the monk,"
we'll be "teaching the elephant nine hundred ways to dance
on the end her trunk."

The "S" Is for Salmonella

Our hostess does not wish to kill,
but the shrimp puffs have an axe to grind.
She served them up. We ate our fill.
Our hostess does not wish to kill.
But the heat of day and lack of dill
have turned the shellfish most unkind.
Our hostess does not wish to kill,
but the shrimp puffs have an axe to grind.

One a Day

Is life merely the sum of all the pills you take?
Or is it what remains once the drugs have left your system?
When you finally stop that snowy night and give your
    harness bells a shake—
is life solely the sum of all the pills you have to take?
And is that number doubled daily by the promises you break?
Or is it factored by the years and how far away you've pissed them?
Life: is it the sum of all the pills you take?
Or is it what takes over once they've gone and left your system?

More T-Shirt Wisdom

What would shooby-dooby do?

What would hair do?

What would Xana du?

What would Katman du?

What would that voodoo that you do do?

What would a kudu do?

What would Rocky II do?

What would that crazy Jew do?

What would the French word for two deux?

What would Cthulu do?

What would that crazy Jew in a muumuu do?

What would Tippecanoe and Tyler too do?

What would Timbuktu do?

Lines Composed in an Alcove a Few Feet Outside of a Public Restroom

Eternity might feel like this
a place between two other places
at far remove from the taste of your kiss

in a rushing stream of stranger's faces.

A Note of Apology

To anyone who has
crashed
burned
cratered
bought it
or otherwise suffered grievous pain
as a direct result
of using any of my varied
and wonderful ideas
for yourself:
I'm sorry.

But,
I told you so
as well.

Cara Seamus et C: Postcard from Spain

for/from HF

Our dear companion
Matisse urged calm
though the birds
were gleeful
having winged
another year in which
the eggs resisted
excessive cracking.

Be just hard
boiled enough and avoid
painting one another into
the corners
he sagely counseled.

They cooed and feathered
their props
across the full stage.

Hello from Madrid also.

Thread of the Real

Poems by Joseph Hutchison
Colorado Poet Laureate

978-0-9713678-5-2

The thread of the real
strings our words like beads
together, loops them
around our lover's neck—
they kiss her when she walks.

Or say it's a line of mindfulness
that curves between differently
grained materials, a strand
of cloudy glue squeezed clear
between inlays of rosewood
and blond bay laurel. . . .

Umbrellas or Else

Poems by J. Diego Frey

978-1-938633-47-8

Chock full of laugh-out-loud poems, *Umbrellas or Else* blurs the line between the absurd and the profound. Poetry will never again be the same.

> *Tell of a self*
> *upended by rain.*
> *And the forest of kelp*
> *that grew up in my brain.*
> *In the night comes your yelp*
> *(as we circle the drain):*
> *"Umbrellas or else—*
> *we will sing it again!"*